COMMUNISM

RUDOLPH T. HEITS

MASON CREST
PHILADELPHIA

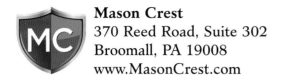

Mason Crest
370 Reed Road, Suite 302
Broomall, PA 19008
www.MasonCrest.com

Printed and bound in the United States of America

CPSIA Compliance Information: Batch #MEG2012-1. For further information, contact Mason Crest at 1-866-MCP-Book.

First printing
1 3 5 7 9 8 6 4 2

Library of Congress Cataloging-in-Publication Data

Heits, Rudolph T.
 Communism / Rudolph T. Heits.
     p. cm. — (Major forms of world government)
 Includes bibliographical references and index.
 ISBN 978-1-4222-2136-5 (hc)
 ISBN 978-1-4222-9453-6 (ebook)
 1. Communism—Juvenile literature. I. Title.
 HX21.H45 2013
 321.9'2—dc23
                              2012027843

Publisher's note: All quotations in this book are taken from original sources, and contain the spelling and grammatical inconsistencies of the original texts.

TITLES IN THIS SERIES

COMMUNISM	MILESTONES	MONARCHY
DEMOCRACY	IN THE EVOLUTION	OLIGARCHY
DICTATORSHIP	OF GOVERNMENT	THEOCRACY
FASCISM		

TABLE OF CONTENTS

INTRODUCTION by Dr. Timothy Colton, Harvard University

When human beings try to understand complex sets of things, they usually begin by sorting them into categories. They classify or group the phenomena that interest them into boxes that are basically very much alike. These boxes can then be compared and analyzed. The logic of classification applies to the study of inanimate objects (such as, for example, bodies of water or minerals), to living organisms (such as species of birds or bacteria), and also to man-made systems (such as religions or communications media).

This series of short books is about systems of government, which are specific and very important kinds of man-made systems. Systems of government are arrangements for human control and cooperation on particular territories. Governments dispense justice, make laws, raise taxes, fight wars, run school and health systems, and perform many other services that we often take for granted. Like, say, minerals, bacteria, and religions, systems of government come in a wide variety of forms or categories.

Just what are those categories? One of the earliest attempts to answer this question rigorously was made in the fourth century BCE by the brilliant Greek philosopher Aristotle. His study *Politics* has come down to us in incomplete form, as many of his writings were lost after he died. Nonetheless, it contains a simple and powerful scheme for classifying systems of government. Aristotle researched and illustrated his treatise by looking at the constitutions of 158 small city-states near the eastern shores of the Mediterranean Sea of his day, most of them inhabited by Greeks.

According to Aristotle's *Politics*, any system of government could be accurately classified and thus understood once two things were known. The first was, how many people were involved in making political decisions: one person, a small number, or a large number. The second issue was whether the system was designed to serve the common good of the citizens of the city-state. Taken together, these distinctions produced six categories of governmental system in all: monarchy (rule by one civic-minded person); tyranny (rule by one selfish person); aristocracy (rule by the few in the interests of all); oligarchy (rule by the few to suit themselves); constitutional government or "polity" (rule by the many in the common interest); and finally a form of mob rule (rule by the many with no concern for the greater good).

The fifth of these classic categories comes closest to modern representative democracy, as it is experienced in the United States, Western Europe, India, and many other places. One of the things Aristotle teaches us, however, is that there are many alternatives to this setup. In addition to the volume on democracy, this Mason Crest series will acquaint students with systems of government that correspond in rough terms to other categories invented by Aristotle more than two thousand years ago. These include monarchy; dictatorship (in Aristotle's terms, tyranny); oligarchy; communism (which we might think of as a particular kind of modern-day oligarchy); fascism (which combines some of the characteristics of tyranny and mob rule); and theocracy (which does not fit easily into Aristotle's scheme, although we might think of it as tyranny or oligarchy, but in the name of some divine being or creed).

Aristotle focused his research on the written constitutions of city-states. Today, political scientists, with better tools at their disposal, delve more into the actual practice of government in different countries. That practice frequently differs from the theory written into the constitution. Scholars study why it is that countries differ so much in terms of how and in whose interests governmental decisions are taken, across broad categories and within these categories, as well as in mixed systems that cross the boundaries between categories. It turns out that there are not one but many reasons for these differences, and there are significant disagreements about which reasons are most important. Some of the reasons are examined in this book series.

Experts on government also wonder a lot about trends over time. Why is it that some version of democracy has come to be the most common form of government in the contemporary world? Why has democratization come in distinct waves, with long periods of stagnation or even of reverse de-democratization separating them? The so-called third wave of democratization began in the 1970s and extended into the 1990s, and featured, among other changes, the collapse of communist systems in the Soviet Union and Eastern Europe and the disintegration of differently constituted nondemocratic systems in Southern Europe and Latin America. At the present time, the outlook for democracy is uncertain. In a number of Arab countries, authoritarian systems of government have recently been overthrown or challenged by revolts. And yet, it is far from clear that the result will be functioning democracies. Moreover, it is far from clear that the world will not encounter another wave of de-democratization. Nor can we rule out the rise of fundamentally new forms of government not foreseen by Aristotle; these might be encouraged by contemporary forms of technology and communication, such as the Internet, behavioral tracking devices, and social media.

For young readers to be equipped to consider complex questions like these, they need to begin with the basics about existing and historical systems of government. It is to meet their educational needs that this book series is aimed.

Mao Zedong casts his ballot in a 1953 election of the National People's Congress, an assembly controlled by the Chinese Communist Party. As chairman of the CCP, Mao ruled the People's Republic of China from 1949 to 1976.

1

NIGHTMARE IN CHINA

Histoy, in the view of the true believers, was leading irresistibly toward a society with no rich and no poor. In such a society, everyone would have enough. In such a society, private property would be abolished. Land would belong to everyone, and factories would be controlled by workers and operated for the benefit of all. In such a society, there would be no social classes. There would be no money. There wouldn't even be a need for government anymore.

A society organized completely around the pursuit of the common good: this was the dream of ardent Communists. It was understood that such a society wouldn't emerge overnight. Still, in

1958, Mao Zedong of China appeared to take a major step toward making that ideal a reality.

PROBLEMS IN A POOR LAND

Mao was the top leader—the chairman—of the Chinese Communist Party (CCP). After World War II, he led the Communists in a revolution that overthrew China's ruling party, the Guomindang. On October 1, 1949, Mao proclaimed the founding of the People's Republic of China (PRC). The PRC would be a Communist state. Governance would be the exclusive right of the CCP. No other political party would be permitted.

The problems facing China's new rulers were huge. With a population of more than 540 million, China was home to more than one-fifth of the world's people. The vast majority lived in poverty. The country had only limited industry, and that was concentrated in a few large cities. Rural areas, where 9 in 10 Chinese resided, were barely touched by modernity. Peasants continued to cultivate the land as they had for centuries. They used hand tools instead of machines for planting and harvesting. They didn't have modern fertilizers to help their crops grow. They didn't have modern irrigation systems to water their crops.

Land ownership was another big problem. Many peasants owned plots of land that were barely large enough to farm profitably. Usually, these peasants could grow just enough to feed their families. In a very good year, they might grow a little extra, which they could sell. But in a year when the weather wasn't great, they faced hunger.

Many other peasants had no land at all. They leased the fields they cultivated. And the rents they paid were quite high. As a result, these peasants stayed in perpetual debt.

Soon after taking power in 1949, China's Communist government started a program of rural land reform. The process involved several steps and took years to complete. By 1956, however, private ownership of land had been eliminated. Individual farms had been merged into "agricultural producers' cooperatives." Each cooperative consisted of about 30 to 50 households.

Many peasants were unhappy about not owning their own land. But because a cooperative's harvest was divided up according to how many hours of labor each family contributed, there were powerful reasons for everyone to work hard.

THE GREAT LEAP FORWARD

In late 1957, Mao Zedong made a bold statement. He said that China should—and could—rapidly become one of the world's leading economic powers. Thus was born the campaign known as the Great Leap Forward. It got under way in 1958.

Mao's plans called for huge gains in agricultural and industrial output. Those gains were supposed to occur in both sectors at the same time.

But China was a poor country. It was only beginning to industrialize. It didn't have very many factories. It didn't have a well-developed system of roads, bridges, canals, or railways along which raw materials, goods, and equipment could move. Its workforce was largely uneducated. With these and other disadvantages, how could China quickly become an economic giant?

This Chinese poster from 1956 describes a 10-year plan for the development of agriculture. The illustrations show Mao Zedong in a meeting, peasants in a field with a poster of Mao, two people with vegetables, and a man on horseback with a herd of horses.

This 1957 poster was designed to rally support for China's industrial policy. It includes images of a manufacturing plant, a map of industrial facilities, and charts showing economic growth. Mao's Great Leap Forward was an ambitious plan for China to catch up economically with industrialized nations like Great Britain and the United States.

Mao looked to rural China for the answer. It had a vast supply of peasant labor. But in Mao's view, these workers weren't being used efficiently. Too many were engaged full time in agriculture. A new way of organizing rural society could change that.

In early 1958, the Chinese government ordered the replacement of agricultural producers' cooperatives with much-larger "people's communes." These would be headed by a manager and a central committee, all of whom were members of the Communist Party. On average, each people's commune comprised around 60 villages and contained about 22,000 people. Each commune was subdivided into village-sized "production brigades." The brigades, in turn, were composed of "production teams" consisting of several dozen households.

This organization, Mao and other CCP officials believed, would allow for flexibility in using the labor force. Workers could be assigned wherever they were most needed at a given time. At planting or harvest time, extra production teams might work in the fields. But at other times, teams could be spared for different tasks. They might do factory work, for example. Or they might mine coal. Sometimes, entire brigades could be deployed on large infrastructure projects. These included the building of roads, dams, and irrigation canals.

If Mao was counting on the commune system to free up labor for industrialization, he also saw other important benefits. He believed the communes would cement peasant loyalty to the Chinese Communist Party. Party cadres—trained and highly motivated members of the CCP—would monitor peasants during virtually every waking hour on the communes. Indoctrination would be constant. Further, Mao viewed the communes as a big step toward the achievement of pure communism. On the communes, workers would control for themselves the means of production—the factories, machinery, tools, and raw materials used to produce goods. There would be no private property. All differences in wealth and status would be eliminated. Most communes even tried to do away with money. But commune members didn't need money. The commune provided everything they needed for free: housing, clothes, food. Children went to commune-run schools. Infants were cared for at commune nurseries so that their mothers could work. The sick received treatment at the commune hospital. To Mao, all this added up to a Communist utopia.

QUESTIONABLE ASSUMPTIONS

By October 1958, more than 25,000 people's communes had been set up all across rural China. And nearly every commune had at least one new factory. The factories had been constructed on land previously used for agriculture. They were kept running by millions of peasants who only months earlier had been full-time farmers. The Great Leap Forward seemed to be off to a good start. In fact, it was on very shaky ground.

Neither Mao nor the other top leaders of the CCP understood much about economics. The Great Leap Forward involved a big assumption: that China could increase its agricultural output using a lot less labor and a lot less land. Under some circumstances, that wouldn't be a completely unreasonable assumption. For example, an investment in tractors, threshers, and other mechanized farm equipment would enable fewer people to do more agricultural work. An investment in modern fertilizers could greatly increase crop yields per acre.

But China didn't make these kinds of investments. Still, Party leaders were confident. Other factors, they believed, would lead to increased grain production. First, there was the revolutionary spirit of the Chinese people. Mao and other Party leaders thought that enthusiasm for communism would spur peasants to higher and higher levels of productivity. Second, China's leaders were counting on new agricultural techniques championed by the Party's "experts." These techniques were supposedly scientific. But they'd never actually been tested.

In both cases, the confidence of China's leaders turned out to be misplaced. Many peasants weren't at all happy about collectivization. But beyond that, there is a limit to the amount of physical labor even highly motivated people can do. Peasants on many communes soon reached that limit. CCP officials didn't help matters by pressing ahead with massive infrastructure projects. Production brigades had to do the backbreaking work of building dams and digging canals with nothing more than picks and shovels. Exhaustion of the labor force added to another problem: the lack of incentives for extra effort. Under the commune system, everyone received the same compensation. And—at least in the beginning of the Great Leap Forward—commune members were promised as much food as they wanted. Under these circumstances, it was human nature for individuals to slack off a bit in the rice paddies and wheat fields.

The new agricultural techniques were based not on science but on wishful thinking. According to the CCP's "experts," a lot more grain could be grown on less land if the grain were very densely planted. Of course, nature doesn't work that way. Plants need adequate space and nutrients to grow.

CATASTROPHE

By the end of 1958, clear signs of trouble had appeared. Crop yields were plummeting all over the country.

Nevertheless, commune managers reported bumper harvests for their communes. In turn, regional Communist Party officials reported huge crop yields for their provinces. After one official announced that his province had doubled its grain production, another claimed that his province had tripled its production. Soon another province was reporting quadruple the previous year's yield. Not to be outdone, another provincial official reported a tenfold increase.

These reports weren't true. The 1958 harvests were actually smaller

> ## KEY IDEA
>
> Means of production refers to the physical factors—other than human labor—that are used to produce goods. These include factories, machinery, tools, and raw materials.

than in previous years. But commune managers and provincial officials were eager to advance their careers. They wanted to exceed the expectations of Party leaders.

From Beijing, China's capital, Mao and the CCP leadership made no attempt to verify the reports coming in from the countryside. The miraculous harvests seemed to prove that the system they had set up was working.

Under the Chinese government's scheme for grain distribution, each commune kept part of what it grew: a base amount that was thought to be enough to feed the commune's members, plus a portion of any surplus. The commune had to turn the rest over to the government. After feeding people in China's cities, the government exported most of the remaining grain. Unfortunately, when a commune manager exaggerated the harvest, some of the grain taken by the government wasn't actually surplus. It was part of the base amount needed to feed commune members.

By early 1959, hunger stalked the Chinese countryside. The weakest people—the elderly and the very young—began dying.

A few Party officials tried to sound a warning. One was China's defense minister, Peng Dehuai. Peng understood the depth of the crisis after touring his native province of Hunan. But Mao Zedong rejected his account of exaggerated harvests and hungry peasants. Peng was stripped of his title and placed under house arrest. He was lucky. Some who questioned the size of the harvest were brutally beaten in what the Party called "struggle sessions." Others were executed as traitors.

Disregarding all reports to the contrary, Mao and the CCP leadership insisted that the commune system was working well. Grain targets for 1959 were kept high.

Again, however, the harvests fell short. Again, commune managers and provincial officials lied. Again, the central government took millions of tons of grain from surpluses that didn't exist.

By this time, famine was widespread. The people's communes, which Mao had dreamed would be Communist utopias, were instead places of intense suffering. In many communal mess halls—where commune members were required to eat their meals—the only food available was "grass soup." And even that thin fare was served just once a day. To survive, people ate whatever else they could get their hands on. They caught insects and boiled tree bark. But it wasn't enough. Peasants collapsed and died by the millions. In many places, survivors were too weak to bury all the dead. Bodies were left to decay in fields and on roadsides where they had fallen.

CCP leaders in Beijing could no longer deny that there were major problems in the countryside. But Mao got the idea that the problems weren't with the commune system itself. He insisted that China's agricultural production had, in fact, increased. Mao blamed disloyal peasants for the food shortages. He said these peasants were hiding grain for their own use. So the Chinese government did nothing to relieve the suffering in the countryside. It continued to take a large portion of the grain harvests. It even increased China's grain exports. To address the rural food shortages, the CCP launched an "anti-hoarding" campaign. Party cadres ransacked peasants' homes. They used a variety of brutal tortures to get peasants to reveal their secret stashes of food. But those stashes didn't exist.

Tens of thousands of starving and desperate people tried to flee their communes. They hoped to find food somewhere else. In most cases, security forces returned runaway peasants to their communes. Some were tortured or beaten to death for their disloyalty. Others were simply left to starve with their neighbors.

The crisis continued through 1960 and 1961. Finally, in early 1962, the CCP quietly changed its agricultural policies. The Chinese government cut back on the amount of grain it took from the communes. It began importing food.

The scale of China's "Great Famine" of 1959–1961 is hard to grasp. Many population experts place the death toll at about 30 million. Some, however, believe the actual number was much higher. In any case, there is broad agreement that the Great Famine was the largest mass starvation ever.

A FLAWED SYSTEM?

History offers many illustrations of the horrors that can be caused by power-hungry, corrupt, or inept leaders. Certainly China's Great Famine is a prime example. That catastrophe would not have occurred without the supremely bad leadership of Mao Zedong. Mao was utterly incompetent when it came to managing China's economy. At the same time, he stubbornly refused to admit his mistakes or change course. He was ruthless in imposing his political will. The Great Famine, then, can be attributed to the failures of a deeply flawed individual who held national power. But many scholars also see it as evidence of the shortcomings of communism as a basis for government.

No form of government is perfect. On occasion serious abuses have been committed, and terrible suffering produced, under every system of government ever tried. Beyond that, no type of government has completely eliminated inefficiency or corruption. No type of government has completely eliminated social and economic problems.

But, as critics have pointed out, the record of Communist governments seems especially dismal. Communism has almost always meant severe restrictions on the freedom of citizens. Worse still, monstrous excesses have been all too common under communism. Among Communist leaders, Mao Zedong is hardly unique in the brutality of his rule.

This wasn't supposed to happen. Communism, according to its intellectual founders, would lead to the fulfillment of human potential. It would set people free.

enabled vastly more goods to be produced, and at a much lower cost, than previously. It also shifted manufacturing from homes and small workshops to large factories. Great numbers of people moved from the countryside, where their labor was no longer needed, to cities and towns. There they hoped to find factory jobs.

The lives of factory workers were extremely difficult. They lived in crowded, disease-filled slums. They were paid very low wages and worked long hours. Even children as young as six toiled through 13- or 14-hour shifts. And factory machines were dangerous. Accidents were common.

By the early 1800s, reformers had begun calling for changes to improve the lives of workers. Some even questioned the economic system that fueled the Industrial Revolution. That economic system was capitalism.

Capitalism is based on economic freedom. Under capitalism, anyone may set up a business or invest money in a business. If the business fails, the owners and investors lose their money. But if it succeeds, they get to keep the profits. Capitalism is also based on competition. Businesses compete with one another to produce goods that people will want to buy. When several businesses produce the same thing, the one that offers

The Industrial Revolution of the 18th and 19th centuries resulted in major changes to societies throughout the world. The introduction of new manufacturing technologies, combined with improvements that made farming more efficient, caused many people to move from rural areas to cities in search of factory jobs. Over time, industrial workers began to organize into labor unions to fight for better pay and safer working conditions.

better quality or a lower price will tend to win out. Workers, too, must compete with one another under capitalism. They compete for jobs. They compete to earn enough money to buy the goods they want. Under pure capitalism, people who don't have enough money to buy what they want—or sometimes even what they need—go without. The early champions of capitalism admitted that this was unfortunate. But they insisted that governments shouldn't interfere with the workings of the free market, where wages and prices are set by the interplay between supply and demand.

Capitalism unleashed tremendous economic growth during the late 18th and early 19th centuries. More goods were produced than ever before. Overall, standards of living rose. But the benefits were very uneven. Some investors and business owners accumulated fortunes. Yet the workers who toiled in their mills and factories lived in desperate poverty.

Some reformers called for governments to pass laws giving workers certain protections. These included limits on the length of the workday. Other reformers said there was a better way to organize economic activity: socialism. This system would be based on cooperation rather than competition. Under socialism, important resources and industries are publicly rather than privately owned. The resources are used and the industries operated not for private profit but for the benefit of all members of the society. Under socialism, goods are supposed to be distributed equitably rather than according to who can pay for them.

Socialism can take many forms. Some early socialists offered radical suggestions. A few said that all the possessions of the rich should be seized and redistributed. Others wanted to abolish private property completely. Some said that national governments should plan and direct

KEY IDEA

Capitalism and socialism are different systems for organizing economic activity. Capitalism is based on private ownership of industries and businesses. Socialism is based on government or communal ownership.

the economy. Others tried socialism on a smaller scale, setting up model communities where everyone worked together voluntarily and shared in the benefits of what they produced.

MANIFESTO

Shortly after settling in Belgium, Karl Marx became involved in a secret organization whose goal was to promote socialism. It was called the League of the Just. The organization's central committee was in London. There were also chapters in France, Switzerland, and Germany. Marx and his friend Friedrich Engels set up a new chapter in Brussels, the capital of Belgium.

The writings of Karl Marx served as a guide for the development of communism as a political system. Yet when Communist governments actually came to power in the Soviet Union and China during the 20th century, many of Marx's assumptions and predictions proved incorrect.

In 1847 the League of the Just was renamed the Communist League. Marx by this time had won a reputation for persuasiveness. The London Central Committee commissioned him to write a pamphlet explaining the principles of the Communist League.

The result was published in February 1848 as *The Manifesto of the Communist Party*. Today it is usually referred to simply as *The Communist Manifesto*. (A manifesto is a declaration of principles.) Marx and Engels were listed as co-authors, but Marx is believed to have done the writing.

In *The Communist Manifesto*, Marx claimed that all of recorded history could be boiled down to a single dynamic: class struggle. By this, Marx meant conflict between the different social classes in a given society. The roots of this conflict were always economic. In simple terms, at every period in recorded history, one class owned the means of production and controlled the labor of others. This ruling class was thus, without actually working, able to take for itself the society's surplus product. (Surplus product refers to the goods produced in excess of what workers and their families need.) Not surprisingly, the workers who produced society's goods weren't happy with this situation. They opposed the ruling class in various ways. Sometimes, class struggle led to the overthrow of the old ruling class and the creation of a new ruling class. At other times changes in the way goods were produced led to changes in the social order.

Class struggle in the modern era, Marx said, was between the bourgeoisie (pronounced boorzh-wah-ZEE) and the proletariat (pro-leh-TARE-ee-it). The bourgeoisie were the property-owning middle class and wealthy capitalists who owned the means of production. The proletariat was the class of industrial workers. They didn't own property or the means of production. Therefore, they had to sell their labor to the bourgeoisie in order to survive.

Marx believed that capitalism contained the seeds of its own destruction. Competition would force more and more people into the ranks of the proletariat. People at the lower levels of the middle class, such as artisans and shopkeepers, would be put out of business first. Later, small-scale factory owners and capitalists would be ruined by big capitalists. Wealth would be concentrated in the hands of an ever-smaller group.

> "THE COMMUNISTS DISDAIN TO CONCEAL THEIR VIEWS AND AIMS. THEY OPENLY DECLARE THAT THEIR ENDS CAN BE ATTAINED ONLY BY THE FORCIBLE OVERTHROW OF ALL EXISTING SOCIAL CONDITIONS. LET THE RULING CLASSES TREMBLE AT A COMMUNISTIC REVOLUTION. THE PROLETARIANS HAVE NOTHING TO LOSE BUT THEIR CHAINS. THEY HAVE A WORLD TO WIN. WORKING MEN OF ALL COUNTRIES, UNITE!"
>
> *—THE COMMUNIST MANIFESTO*

Meanwhile, the masses of people would live in misery. They would earn only enough money to keep themselves alive and able to continue working. Eventually, the members of the proletariat would be united by their awful plight. They would rise up and violently overthrow the bourgeoisie.

There would follow a period of transition that Marx later referred to as the "dictatorship of the proletariat." During this period, capitalism would be permanently destroyed. The means of production would be transferred from the bourgeoisie to the proletariat. Inherited wealth would be abolished. A form of socialism would be established. In this socialism, the state—now controlled by the proletariat—would own all factories and other places of work. Wages and the distribution of goods would still be somewhat unequal. But that would be temporary.

After the right conditions had been created, human society would move to the final stage in its historical development: communism. All class distinctions would be gone. All private property would be abolished. People would live in harmony. Each person would contribute to society according to his or her ability. Each would receive according to his or her need. There would be no reason for government anymore. So, in the words of Friedrich Engels, the state itself would "wither away."

WAITING FOR THE REVOLUTION

Marx ended *The Communist Manifesto* by urging industrial workers in all countries to unite. He wanted to get the revolution to overthrow capitalism started. But he believed that in the long run, it really didn't matter what he did. After a society reached an advanced stage of industrialization, Marx thought, its exploited and impoverished workers would inevitably rise up. Socialism would inevitably follow. And communism was the inevitable end result of historical development.

Marx was thrilled when events seemed to confirm his ideas. In 1848, revolutions broke out all across Europe. The first, in France, came the very week *The Communist Manifesto* was published. Unrest soon spread to Marx's native Prussia, to Austria, and to the states of Italy. Uprisings in Hungary and the German kingdoms of Saxony and Bavaria followed.

An angry Prussian mob breaks into the government arsenal in Berlin, June 1848. The previous March, a revolutionary wave had spread throughout the German-speaking states of central Europe as people demanded government reforms and greater freedom. The revolutionaries were encouraged by editorials and stories in *Neue Rheinische Zeitung* ("New Rhenish Newspaper"), published by Karl Marx and other early Communists.

In the end, however, most of the revolutions were put down. A general uprising by the proletariat never materialized.

In 1849 Marx fled to London. He would remain in England for the rest of his life. He devoted himself to the "scientific study" of capitalism. He wrote several books, including the massive *Capital*. In it, Marx expanded his ideas about how capitalism works.

Marx continued to believe that it was only a matter of time before the proletariat rose up and overthrew the bourgeoisie. But he died on March 15, 1883, without ever seeing a proletarian revolution happen.

3

RISE OF THE USSR

Karl Marx had predicted that the first successful proletarian revolution would occur in a wealthy, highly industrialized country. He was wrong. It took place in a poor country with a mostly agrarian economy. That country was Russia.

OPPOSING THE TSAR

From the early 1600s, Russia had been ruled by the Romanov dynasty. Its tsars, or emperors, wielded enormous power. Often, their rule was highly repressive. By the 1800s, a force of secret police was established. It ferreted out Russians who opposed the tsar. When found, these people were punished harshly.

During the last decades of the 19th century, the ideas of Marx began to gain currency among certain anti-tsarist intellectuals. One such person was a young lawyer born Vladimir Ilyich Ulyanov in 1870. History remembers him better by an alias: Lenin. In 1895 he cofounded a Marxist group, called the League of Struggle for the Emancipation of the Working Class, in the Russian capital of St. Petersburg. Lenin's attempts to organize industrial workers led to his arrest. After a year in jail, he was exiled to remote Siberia.

In 1898 leaders of several small Marxist groups met in the city of Minsk. They formed the Russian Social Democratic Labor Party (RSDLP). A crackdown by tsarist police soon forced RSDLP leaders into exile in Europe.

Lenin, after completing his Siberian exile in 1900, also went to Europe. There he joined the RSDLP. In 1903 the RSDLP held a party congress in London. At the congress, a dispute between Lenin and another party leader produced a rift in the RSDLP. Two factions, the Mensheviks and the Bolsheviks, emerged. Lenin was the acknowledged head of the more radical Bolsheviks.

Back in Russia, the tsar's regime would soon face difficulties. In February 1904, Russia went to war with Japan. The Russian forces suffered one defeat after another. This began to shake confidence in the tsar. Then, on January 22, 1905, factory workers in St. Petersburg organized a demonstration. They planned to march to the Winter Palace. There they would present Tsar Nicholas II with a petition. It called for an end to the war with Japan, as well as reforms such as the right to vote and improved conditions for factory workers. The demonstrators

The uprising that overthrew Tsar Nicholas II was known in the Soviet Union as the February Revolution, even though it occurred in March 1917. Similarly, the revolution that brought the Bolsheviks to power in November 1917 is referred to as the October Revolution. The reason? Russia had not yet adopted the modern, or Gregorian, calendar. The old Julian calendar was about 13 days behind.

were peaceful. But the tsar's Imperial Guard fired on them. Hundreds were killed or wounded.

The massacre of "Bloody Sunday" triggered massive unrest throughout the Russian Empire. Later in the year, Tsar Nicholas was forced to accept certain reforms. For example, a parliament, called the Duma, was set up. Also, a constitution was written and approved in 1906. It affirmed the basic human rights of all Russians. Still, the document left little doubt that the tsar would continue to hold near-absolute power. "The supreme autocratic power is vested in the Tsar of all the Russias," the constitution stated. "It is God's command that his authority should be obeyed not only through fear but for conscience sake."

THE RUSSIAN REVOLUTION

Little more than a decade would pass before the tsar's authority was swept away completely. Again, it was a war that stoked the discontent of the Russian people.

That war is known today as World War I. It began in August 1914. Russia joined its major allies, Great Britain and France, in fighting against Germany, Austria-Hungary, and the Ottoman Empire. All sides suffered terrible numbers of casualties. But Russia was dreadfully unprepared for the war. Its army didn't even have enough rifles to go around. Its commanders were inept. As a result, the Russian army was beaten again and again, especially by the Germans.

By 1917 Russians were sick of the war. Soldiers didn't want to fight anymore. On the home front, food was scarce. Unemployment was high. Prices skyrocketed. Many people blamed Tsar Nicholas.

In March, worker strikes shut down factories in St. Petersburg, which had been renamed Petrograd in 1914. Petrograd was where much of Russia's military equipment was produced. Widespread demonstrations and rioting broke out across the city. Tsar Nicholas ordered the army to put down the unrest. But the soldiers refused. Many soldiers joined the protesters. On March 15, the tsar officially gave up his throne.

The following day, a temporary government was announced. The Provisional Government included members of the Duma. They championed liberal reforms. They wanted Russia to be a parliamentary republic. The Provisional Government supported the creation of local dumas. These elected councils would bring self-rule to towns and villages across Russia.

But the Provisional Government didn't hold complete power. In Petrograd there was another powerful council. It was called the Petrograd Soviet. It claimed to represent the interests of workers and soldiers. Its deputies were members of various socialist parties. Soon other soviets were being set up in towns and cities across Russia.

Joseph Stalin, a Bolshevik leader, came out in support of both the Provisional Government and the Petrograd Soviet. It seemed that the Provisional Government and the Petrograd Soviet might be able to exist side by side.

That changed in April, when Lenin returned to Russia from Switzerland. He argued against cooperation with the Provisional Government. Lenin didn't want Russia to be a "bourgeois" parliamentary republic. He wanted communism. To achieve that, he called for a revolution. He wanted the Bolshevik Party to lead Russia's industrial workers and peasants in overthrowing the Provisional Government.

But the Bolsheviks were a minority in the Petrograd Soviet. And Lenin didn't win over Russia's other socialist parties. They rejected his call for the overthrow of the Provisional Government. Soon, socialist parties were brought into the Provisional Government.

The Provisional Government had many problems. Russia was still fighting in World War I. And the war effort continued to go badly. Unrest in Russia grew.

By late summer, the Bolsheviks had gained a majority in the Petrograd Soviet. The Provisional Government, meanwhile, had scheduled elections for mid-November. The voting would be to select members of a new Constituent Assembly. Lenin decided to make a decisive move before the elections took place.

Vladimir Lenin addresses a crowd during the 1917 Russian Revolution. Lenin (1870–1924) adapted the theories of Karl Marx to create a form of communism that could be implemented in Russia.

On November 6–7, forces loyal to the Bolsheviks took control of Petrograd. There was little fighting. By this time, most Russian soldiers in the city favored the Petrograd Soviet. Members of the Provisional Government were arrested at the Winter Palace.

Immediately afterward, representatives of Russia's socialist parties met at what was called the Second All-Russian Congress of Soviets. Bolsheviks made up about half of the 650 delegates. Lenin put forth a pair of decrees. One called for an end to the war. The other called for the redistribution of land. The estates of the wealthy, monasteries of the Russian Orthodox Church, and the holdings of the Romanovs would all be transferred to workers' and peasants' soviets. Both decrees were approved. The congress also approved a temporary government. It would rule until the Constituent Assembly was up and running. The temporary government was called the Council of People's Commissars (CPC). It was controlled by the Bolsheviks but included members of other socialist parties. Lenin was the CPC's chairman.

The world's first Communist government had come to power. But gaining power and holding it would be two different matters.

CIVIL WAR

The Bolsheviks failed to get a majority in the elections for Russia's Constituent Assembly. They received just under 24 percent of the vote. The Socialist Revolutionary Party got the largest share of the votes, with 40 percent.

But Lenin had no intention of sharing power. In late December, he set up a secret police organization to eliminate opponents. It was known as the Cheka. In January 1918, Lenin dissolved the Constituent Assembly after it had met just once. This angered Russians of all political persuasions, including members of socialist parties. A peace treaty with Germany, signed in March, also was unpopular. In that treaty, Russia gave up a lot of territory.

By the early summer of 1918, Russia was embroiled in a full-scale civil war. It pitted the Bolsheviks, or "Reds," against a loose coalition known as the "Whites." The Whites included moderate socialists, liberal democrats, and people who wanted to see a return of monarchical rule. The Whites received support from France, Great Britain, the United States, and Japan. A small number of British and U.S. soldiers even fought the Bolshevik Red Army in northwestern Russia during 1918 and 1919.

By late 1920, the civil war was over. The Reds had won.

EARLY YEARS OF THE USSR

Russia was now known as the Russian Soviet Federative Socialist Republic (RSFSR). It was firmly under the control of the Russian Communist Party, as the Bolshevik Party had been renamed. All other parties were outlawed. Members of the Communist Party held all positions at every level of government. The Party itself was controlled by its Central Committee. Lenin was its head.

Lenin was deeply influenced by Marx. But he still understood that he would have to adapt Marx's thinking to conditions in the RSFSR. Marx described the "dictatorship of the proletariat" in somewhat vague terms. Marxism didn't really provide a blueprint for governing. So Lenin added to and adapted Marx's ideas, creating what became known as Marxism-Leninism.

One of the biggest issues was how best to organize the economy. During the civil war, Lenin had instituted what was called "War Communism." Under War Communism, the government took crops directly from the peasants. In the cities, food was rationed. The government brought all industry and domestic and foreign trade under its control. It banned free enterprise.

War Communism caused great hardships for the Russian people. Many peasants resisted. Famine broke out. At the same time, industrial production fell calamitously.

In 1921 Lenin decided to replace War Communism with the New Economic Policy. It marked the return to a limited sort of capitalism. Small businesses and industries were again allowed to operate for profit. Peasants were allowed to keep or sell much more of the crops they grew. The state continued to control finance and bigger industries.

Lenin hoped the New Economic Policy would allow the economy to recuperate. Then communism could be instituted. His hopes were largely realized. Under the New Economic Policy, the economy did recover.

On December 30, 1922, the Union of Soviet Socialist Republics (USSR) was created. It united the RSFSR with the Ukrainian Soviet Socialist Republic, the Byelorussian Soviet Socialist Republic, and the Transcaucasian Soviet Federal Socialist Republic. Over the next two decades, as a result of political reorganization and conquest, the USSR—which was also called the Soviet Union—would come to include 15 soviet socialist republics (SSRs).

This photograph of Lenin and his deputy Joseph Stalin (1879–1953) was taken in 1922, the year the Union of Soviet Socialist Republics (USSR) was formed. After Lenin's death, Stalin emerged from a struggle for power as the USSR's sole ruler.

By late 1922, Lenin had suffered a pair of strokes. Partially paralyzed, he withdrew from his leadership role. A third stroke, in March 1923, left him confined to a bed and unable to speak. He died on January 21, 1924.

Lenin hadn't named a successor. Power in the Soviet Union would eventually fall to one of the most ruthless dictators in history.

THE ERA OF STALIN

Joseph Stalin had been appointed general secretary of the Communist Party's Central Committee in 1922. This was a seemingly unimportant position. But Stalin found ways to use it to build his power, and in particular his power over the selection of people who worked in the Soviet government at all levels. After Lenin's death in January 1924, he moved to shore up his power. One by one, he had potential rivals removed from their posts. Some were expelled from the Party. Some, like Leon Trotsky, were forced into exile abroad. By no later than 1928, Stalin was firmly in charge.

Stalin abandoned the New Economic Policy in 1928. He got rid of limited capitalism. Instead, he brought the entire economy under the control of the state. Everyone would work for, and be paid by, the state. Stalin introduced central planning. From the Kremlin in Moscow, which had been made the national capital in 1918, a committee of Soviet economic planners directed which goods would be produced in the country. They allotted the required resources. They determined how finished goods would be distributed and how much those goods would cost. Central planning was carried out through Five-Year Plans. These set the Soviet Union's development priorities and goals for a five-year period. The first one was

> **KEY IDEA**
>
> Marxism-Leninism is the Communist theory created through Lenin's adaptation of Karl Marx's ideas. One important idea of Lenin's was that the proletariat wouldn't inevitably rise up against capitalism. In Lenin's view, a small party of professional revolutionaries was needed to lead the proletariat, in alliance with revolutionary peasants.

The word *soviet* originally referred to an elected council representing workers.

adopted in 1928. It focused on rapid industrialization and called for big increases in the production of steel, coal, oil, electricity, and weapons.

The goals of the First Five-Year Plan were met a year early. But this success came at a huge human cost. Stalin had ordered the creation of huge collective farms. He wanted to increase agricultural output. But he also wanted to destroy the class of relatively well-off peasants known as kulaks. Stalin thought the kulaks were disloyal to communism.

Many peasants were unhappy about losing their land. Collectivization was carried out by force. Those who resisted faced a harsh fate. Some were executed. Many more were resettled in other regions of the Soviet Union. Still others were sent to the gulag. This was a network of forced-labor prison camps. Most of the camps were located in cold and remote Siberia.

The disorder brought about by Stalin's collectivization campaign caused food production to fall. Famine broke out in Russia, part of the Transcaucus region, and other areas. Several million people died of starvation or disease.

Famine also broke out in the Ukraine. But some historians believe it wasn't an unintended result of collectivization. Rather, they say, it was deliberate. According to these historians, Stalin was concerned that some Ukrainians might want independence. So he ordered the seizure of vast amounts of grain from the Ukrainian SSR to cause mass starvation. In 1932–33, perhaps 5 million Ukrainians died as a result.

In the late 1930s, Stalin again focused his attention on getting rid of potential opponents of his rule. He launched the Great Purge. The Soviet secret police, which at this time was called the NKVD, arrested many prominent members of the Communist Party. It also arrested many top military leaders. These people were accused of all sorts of plots against the Soviet government. Under torture, many confessed. Often they pointed the finger at other supposed traitors.

Few, if any, of the plots had even a small basis in reality. The NKVD had simply made them up. But it didn't matter. The accused were condemned, some of them at show trials. Many were executed. Others were sent to the gulag.

Even after leaders in the Communist Party and military had been eliminated, the Great Purge continued. It swept up an ever-widening circle of ordinary Soviet citizens. Under questioning by the NKVD, people accused acquaintances, friends, and even family members of disloyalty to the government. Everyone lived in terror. And that was the idea. No one dared oppose Stalin.

The Great Purge lasted from late 1936 to late 1938. The number of victims is unknown. Estimates of the number of people killed range from about 700,000 to 1.2 million. Millions more were imprisoned.

This Soviet propaganda poster from 1931 encourages farmers to embrace collectivization and gather the harvest for the good of the Soviet state. According to Communist ideology, the demands of the state (in this case, the Soviet Union) supersede the needs of individuals. The slogan in Cyrillic reads, "The fight for the Bolshevik harvesting of the crop is the fight for socialism."

Stalin had created a totalitarian state. The government tried to control every aspect of citizens' lives. Later Communist countries would follow suit.

WORLD WAR II

By the late 1930s, Europe was moving closer and closer to war. Led by Adolf Hitler, Nazi Germany had become increasingly aggressive.

On August 23, 1939, the Soviet Union and Nazi Germany signed an agreement. Officially it was called the Treaty of Nonaggression Between Germany and the Union of Soviet Socialist Republics. In the treaty, the two countries pledged not to fight each other for a period of 10 years. Hitler was planning to launch an invasion of Poland. Great Britain and France had warned that this would lead them to declare war on Germany. Hitler wanted to make sure the Soviet Union didn't join the British and French.

In return for the Soviet pledge to stay out of any fighting, Germany made secret promises. It promised to allow the Soviet Union to occupy eastern Poland. It also promised to allow the Soviet Union to take over three countries in the Baltic Sea region. Those countries were Estonia, Latvia, and Lithuania.

On September 1, 1939, Germany invaded Poland. France and Britain declared war on Germany. World War II had begun.

In mid-September, the Soviet Red Army invaded eastern Poland. This territory was added to the Ukrainian and Belorussian Soviet Socialist Republics. In June 1940 Soviet forces occupied the Baltic states. Estonia, Latvia, and Lithuania were incorporated into the USSR. Lands seized from Romania became the Moldavian SSR.

Unfortunately for the Soviet Union, Nazi Germany didn't honor the nonaggression pact. On June 22, 1941, more than 3.5 million German and Nazi-allied troops attacked the USSR. Caught by surprise, Soviet forces were sent reeling by the massive invasion.

In 1919 the Communist International, or Comintern, was founded in Moscow. This organization sought to bring together Communist movements around the world. The Comintern's stated goal was to fight, "by all available means, including armed force, for the overthrow of the international bourgeoisie and for the creation of an international Soviet republic as a transition stage to the complete abolition of the State." The Comintern would last until 1943, when it was dissolved amid World War II.

Soviet foreign minister Vyacheslav Molotov signs the German-Soviet nonaggression pact, August 1939. Among those standing behind Molotov are German foreign minister Joachim von Ribbentrop and Soviet ruler Joseph Stalin. The agreement emboldened the Soviet Union to invade eastern Poland and the Baltic states in 1939 and 1940.

By year's end, Hitler's forces had reached the outskirts of Leningrad (the former Petrograd) and Moscow. The USSR teetered on the edge of defeat. But the Red Army held.

The tide of the fighting turned in favor of the Soviets in 1942. In August, the Germans attacked Stalingrad (now called Volgograd), an industrial city on the Volga River. In brutal fighting, the city was leveled. Both sides suffered horrendous casualties. But by February 1943, the German forces were defeated.

Over the next two years, the Red Army relentlessly pushed the German army back. Meanwhile, British, American, and other Allied forces fought and defeated the Germans in North Africa, Italy, and then France. They advanced on Germany from the west as the Soviets advanced on Germany from the east. In late April 1945, the Red Army entered Berlin, Germany's capital. After two weeks of bloody street battles, Soviet forces were in control of the city. The war in Europe officially ended on May 8 with Germany's surrender.

In the more than two decades since the Soviet Union's founding, only one other Communist state—the Mongolian People's Republic—had been established. That had occurred in 1924, through the military intervention of the Soviet Red Army. But in the aftermath of World War II, communism spread rapidly. By 1950 there were 10 more Communist states.

4

EXPANSION

In February 1945, during the waning days of the fight against Nazi Germany, the leaders of the three principal Allied nations met in Yalta, a resort on the Black Sea coast of Ukraine. President Franklin D. Roosevelt of the United States, Prime Minister Winston Churchill of the United Kingdom, and Premier Joseph Stalin of the USSR discussed how Europe would be restructured after the war was over. They affirmed "the right of all people to choose the form of government under which they will live." In keeping with that principle, the three leaders agreed that free elections would be held as soon as possible in countries that had been under Nazi occupation, as well as in countries that had sided with the Axis (Nazi Germany and its allies).

Stalin went back on this pledge, however. He wasn't interested in self-determination, especially for the peoples of Eastern Europe. Rather, he wanted the countries of the region to have Communist governments that would reliably follow policies set by the Soviet Union. Little stood in the way of Stalin's achieving this aim. The Red Army occupied most of Eastern Europe at the conclusion of World War II. Where necessary, Communist regimes would be installed and sustained by force.

CREATION OF THE EASTERN BLOC

By 1949 Communist rule had been established in Albania, Bulgaria, Czechoslovakia, East Germany, Hungary, Poland, Romania, and Yugoslavia. The specific circumstances that brought Communist regimes to power in these countries varied. In general, however, the process followed a similar course. At first, a veneer of democracy was maintained. There were multiple political parties. Elections were held. But behind the scenes, Soviet authorities directed the local Communist parties. Soviet occupation forces also helped eliminate opponents of communism through violence, intimidation, and imprisonment. When voters chose noncommunist candidates, election results were falsified or overturned. Eventually, Communist parties were in control and opposition parties banned. This basic pattern describes how Bulgaria, East Germany, Hungary, Poland, and Romania became Communist states dominated by the Soviet Union.

In Czechoslovakia, events unfolded a bit differently. For a few years, the Kremlin permitted a coalition of socialist parties to govern with a moderate degree of autonomy. But in 1948, amid signs of a growing spirit of independence in Czechoslovakia, Moscow sponsored a coup that brought Communists to power.

On the other hand, Communists didn't need the Soviet military to gain power in Albania or Yugoslavia. In both countries, Communist partisans had fought invading Axis troops during World War II. The Communists emerged from the war in a strong military position, and they enjoyed considerable popular support. In early 1946, Communist "people's republics" were declared in Albania and Yugoslavia. The regimes in both countries followed Marxist-Leninist doctrine. Initially, they were also both allied with the Soviet Union.

But Yugoslavia's leader, Josip Broz Tito, had a falling-out with Stalin in 1948. Thereafter Yugoslavia, while remaining a Communist state, wouldn't be aligned with the USSR.

Still, by the late 1940s Soviet-dominated "satellite" countries covered Eastern Europe. Collectively these Communist countries were known as the Eastern bloc.

COLD WAR

American policy makers had watched with alarm as the Soviet Union consolidated its hold on Eastern Europe. Officials in Washington feared that Moscow's ambitions didn't end with the Eastern bloc. They believed the Kremlin was bent on exporting communism around the globe. For their part, Soviet leaders thought the United States wanted to isolate the USSR and, ultimately, to extinguish communism.

To a certain degree, this mutual distrust stemmed from the natural opposition between the ideologies of communism and capitalism. Adherents of the former system said that workers' revolutions would inevitably overthrow and replace the latter system. And these revolutions wouldn't be confined within national boundaries. Rather, they would have a global character. This implied that, in the long run, there could be no peaceful coexistence between Communist countries and capitalist countries. "It must not be imagined that the working class in one country or in several countries will march towards socialism and still more to communism while the capitalists of other countries sit still with folded arms and look on with indifference," Stalin had told a delegation of American trade-union members visiting the Soviet Union in 1927.

> Nor must it be imagined that the working class in capitalist countries will agree to be mere spectators of the victorious development of socialism in one or another country. As a matter of fact, the capitalists will do all in their power to crush such countries. . . . [I]n the further progress of development of the international

revolution, two world centers will be formed: the socialist center, attracting to itself all the countries gravitating towards socialism, and the capitalist center, attracting to itself all the countries gravitating towards capitalism. The fight between these two centers for the conquest of world economy will decide the fate of capitalism and communism throughout the whole world, for the final defeat of world capitalism means the victory of socialism in the arena of world economy.

In the late 1940s, a struggle did emerge between the world centers of capitalism and communism—led by the United States and the USSR, respectively. But that struggle, known as the Cold War, didn't play out quite as Stalin had predicted. To begin, it wasn't conducted mainly in "the arena of world economy." Rather, it was primarily a political and military contest. The Cold War was, however, every bit as significant as the showdown Stalin anticipated in 1927. It defined international politics for four decades. And, to a great extent, it decided the fate of communism as a workable form of governance.

Today, historians disagree about many key questions surrounding the start of the Cold War. Some argue that Soviet leaders wanted to avoid a conflict with the United States. These historians believe that Stalin had no immediate territorial ambitions beyond securing Eastern Europe. That would create a buffer against another invasion of the USSR. Other historians, however, believe that the Soviets were determined to spread communism wherever they could, and by any means necessary.

Whatever the case, American officials took the latter view. They put in place policies to contain Soviet expansion. One important measure was the commitment of hundreds of millions of dollars in economic and military aid to Greece and Turkey. In 1946 a civil war had broken out in Greece when Communists attempted to take over the government. They were supported by the Communist regimes in neighboring Yugoslavia, Bulgaria, and Albania, though not directly by the USSR. Turkey, meanwhile, was under Soviet pressure to surrender control of a strategic waterway, the Dardanelles. In March 1947 U.S. president Harry Truman gave a speech before Congress in which he requested aid for Greece and Turkey. In that speech, he expressed what came to be called the Truman Doctrine. "[I]t must be the policy of the United States," Truman said, "to support free peoples who are resisting attempted subjugation by armed minorities or by outside pressures." The armed minorities and outside pressures to which the president referred were, of course, Communists.

In 1948 the United States began another program to prevent the spread of communism. A multibillion-dollar effort to rebuild the war-torn economies of Western Europe, it was known as the Marshall Plan. A military alliance to defend Western Europe against possible Soviet aggression was set up in 1949. Called the North Atlantic Treaty Organization (NATO), it included the United States, the United Kingdom, France, Belgium, Luxembourg, the Netherlands, Canada, Portugal, Italy, Norway, Denmark, and Iceland.

The Soviet Union moved to counter NATO in 1955. That year, Moscow spearheaded the creation of the Warsaw Pact. This alliance included the USSR, Albania, Bulgaria, Czechoslovakia, East Germany, Hungary, Poland, and Romania.

COMMUNISM IN ASIA

Communism would never gain a foothold in Western Europe. The same could not be said of Asia.

To the great alarm of American policy makers, the world's most populous country became a Communist state in October 1949, after a long rural insurgency. And within five months, the People's Republic of China had announced a formal alliance with the Soviet Union.

In April 1950 the Communist dictator of North Korea, Kim Il-sung, traveled to Moscow. He asked Joseph Stalin to approve an invasion of South Korea. Stalin agreed. Kim then apparently sought and obtained the approval of Chinese leader Mao Zedong.

Korea, a colony of Japan from 1910 to 1945, had been divided at the 38th parallel of latitude at the end of World War II. The division, agreed to by the United States and the USSR, wasn't supposed to be permanent. But Soviet and American officials were unable to agree on the makeup of a provisional government that would prepare a unified Korea for independence.

Yugoslavia's Communist leader, Marshal Josip Broz Tito, shakes hands with Soviet premier Nikita Khrushchev (black suit) at a 1960 meeting. During the Cold War, Yugoslavia attempted to follow a neutral and independent course, turning down invitations to join both the American-led North Atlantic Treaty Organization (NATO) and the Soviet-led Warsaw Pact military alliance.

In the north, the USSR installed Kim. In the South, the anticommunist strongman Syngman Rhee came to power with U.S. backing. Both regimes claimed to be the legitimate government of Korea.

On June 25, 1950, North Korean forces launched a massive invasion. U.S. and United Nations troops rushed to defend South Korea. By year's end, China had also entered the conflict, with the Soviet Union providing secret air support. The war ground to a bloody stalemate. When the fighting ended in July 1953, the border between North and South Korea was again around the 38th parallel, where it had been when the war started.

In the meantime, another war involving Communist forces raged in Southeast Asia. This conflict was in Vietnam.

France had made Vietnam a colony in the 1880s. But during World War II the Japanese army had invaded and, eventually, thrown out the French colonial administration. Armed resistance to the Japanese occupation had been spearheaded by the Viet Minh. This group, led by a seasoned revolutionary named Ho Chi Minh, was composed largely but not entirely of Communists.

COMMUNISM AND DEMOCRACY

Communist countries have typically claimed to be democratic. But while they may have elections, that doesn't make them democracies.

When the Communist Party is the only legal political party, voters have limited choice at best. For instance, in the USSR up until 1987, citizens voted for members of their local or national soviet. But only one Communist Party–approved candidate would be on the ballot.

Communist states usually justify the dominance of the Communist Party by claiming that it alone represents the interests of workers or the will of the people. Only a minority of citizens are members of the Communist Party (usually under 10 percent). But in most Communist states, Party membership is open to anyone who meets certain requirements.

In Communist states, "democratic centralism" prevails within the Party itself. This idea was first described by Lenin. It says that free and open discussion can occur when the Party is considering a decision. However, once the matter has been voted on, there can be no further discussion. Everyone must obey without questioning.

On September 2, 1945—the day Japan formally surrendered to the Allied Powers—Ho Chi Minh proclaimed Vietnam's independence. French officials had other ideas, however. Soon about 35,000 French troops landed in Vietnam. Their mission was to bring Vietnam under the control of France once again.

Ho Chi Minh had been a Communist for a quarter century. But he was also a nationalist. In fact, he seems to have been far more concerned about gaining nationhood for the Vietnamese people than about following Marxist doctrine. In February 1946 Ho sent a telegram to President Truman. In it he appealed for the United States to restrain the French and support Vietnamese independence. Although the United States had affirmed the principle that all peoples have the right to choose the form of government under which they will live, Ho's plea for American intervention went unanswered.

In late 1946, fighting broke out between French forces and the Viet Minh. In 1954, after a long and bloody guerrilla campaign, the Vietnamese won a decisive victory.

However, in the peace agreement that followed, Vietnam was divided. As in Korea, the division was supposed to be temporary. National elections to unify the country were to be held in 1956. But those elections never took place. In large measure, that was because the Communists would have won, and U.S. policy makers weren't about to let that happen. They feared that if Vietnam were allowed to become a Communist state, all of Southeast Asia would inevitably fall to communism. President Dwight D. Eisenhower created a memorable image to illustrate this fear.

"You have a row of dominoes set up," Eisenhower said, "you knock over the first one, and what will happen to the last one is the certainty that it will go over very quickly. So you could have a beginning of a disintegration that would have the most profound influences."

Following the so-called domino theory, the United States propped up an unpopular anticommunist government in South Vietnam. Ho Chi Minh, meanwhile, was president of Communist North Vietnam. In the late 1950s, however, Communist guerrillas supported by North Vietnam began fighting to overthrow the South

Bust of the Vietnamese Communist leader Ho Chi Minh in front of the national flag.

COMMUNIST STATES

About two-dozen Communist states have existed, at one time or another. Communist states have several distinguishing characteristics:

- They are single-party states. This means that rule is achieved through the Communist Party, and only the Communist Party has the right to rule. Generally all other political parties are banned.

- The Communist Party and the state are very closely linked. Usually the state is little more than an extension of the Party.

- The government claims to follow the ideas of Marxism-Leninism, usually with modifications for the country's unique situation.

- The state controls the national economy to a great extent. Typically, officials in the national government (who are also Communist Party leaders) decide which goods will be produced, and they allocate the required resources. Such an economy is called a command economy.

Vietnamese regime. The United States gradually was drawn into an active role in defending South Vietnam. By 1968 more than half a million American troops were fighting the Communist guerrillas as well as North Vietnam's regular army. In 1973 the United States finally pulled its combat forces out of Vietnam. The government of South Vietnam fell two years later, and all of Vietnam came under Communist rule.

The year 1975 saw Communist groups seize power in two of Vietnam's neighbors. In Laos, it was the Pathet Lao, or Lao People's Front. In Cambodia, it was the Khmer Rouge. Both groups had received military support from North Vietnam.

The Khmer Rouge ruled Cambodia from 1975 to 1979. Their four-year reign ranks as one of the most appalling periods in the annals of communism. For sheer brutality, Cambodia's Communist regime was every bit the equal of Stalin's in the 1930s or Mao's in the late 1950s and early

1960s, during China's disastrous Great Leap Forward. The Khmer Rouge killed an estimated 1.7 million people—perhaps one-quarter of Cambodia's total population—through execution, torture, starvation, and forced labor. This genocide was committed in the name of transforming Cambodia into what Khmer Rouge leaders imagined to be a pure Communist state.

CUBA AND THE MISSILE CRISIS

A Communist state had been established in America's own backyard by the early 1960s. In January 1959 a guerrilla force led by Fidel Castro ousted Cuban dictator Fulgencio Batista. Like Ho Chi Minh in Vietnam, Castro during the insurgency had appealed mostly to his fellow Cubans' sense of nationalism. In December 1960, however, the Cuban government came out in support of Soviet policies. It seemed clear that Castro intended to bring Marxism-Leninism to his country.

Even before Castro publicly aligned his regime with the USSR, the United States had begun secretly training Cuban exiles for an invasion of the island. In April 1961 the exiles landed at the Bay of Pigs in southwestern Cuba. They were quickly defeated. In the aftermath, Cuba became a close ally of the Soviet Union.

In 1962 Castro agreed to allow the Soviets to place missiles in Cuba. The missiles were capable of carrying nuclear warheads. Since Cuba is just 90 miles south of Florida, a devastating nuclear attack could be launched against the United States with almost no warning. For a few tense weeks in October 1962, the United States and the Soviet Union appeared to be on the brink of war. But in the end, Nikita Khrushchev—who had taken over as the USSR's top leader after the death of Stalin in 1953—decided to remove the missiles.

Cuba remained a close ally of the Soviet Union and attempted to spread communism in Latin America as well as Africa. During the 1970s and 1980s, Cuban troops were stationed in several African countries to support Marxist movements or governments there. These countries included Angola, Ethiopia, Mozambique, and Somalia.

5

DECLINE

Throughout most of the Cold War, people in the West tended to see communism as a unified front. Communists across the globe, in this view, pursued a single-minded agenda. That agenda involved overthrowing capitalist liberal democracies everywhere and, ultimately, establishing an international socialist order. It was broadly assumed that the Kremlin orchestrated this worldwide Communist movement. Behind every Marxist party, behind every socialist-leaning leader in any country, lurked the Soviet Union.

The USSR did, in fact, support a host of Marxist-Leninist revolutionaries around the world. It did provide economic and military aid to various Communist regimes. It did hold—for a time, at least—the leading role in shaping Communist ideology.

Nevertheless, the Cold War notion of monolithic, Moscow-directed "world communist movement" was a myth. The reality was much more complicated. Marxist-Leninist revolutions were molded by unique national circumstances. Similarly, the character of Communist regimes across the world varied. Individual leaders or governments, even as they accepted aid from the USSR, often made strategic calculations independently of the Kremlin. Some sought to modify the Soviet model. Others broke with the USSR entirely.

TROUBLES IN EASTERN EUROPE

Cracks in the Eastern bloc emerged by 1956. On June 28 of that year, factory workers in the Polish city of Poznan began demonstrating for better pay and working conditions. Other citizens of Poznan who were disillusioned with communism soon joined the factory workers. Rioting broke out. Poland's minister of defense, a Soviet general named Konstantin Rokossovsky, dispatched more than 10,000 troops to quell the unrest. The soldiers did so, but there was considerable bloodshed. Protests spread to other cities. Anger toward the Soviet Union was unmistakable.

Poland's Communist rulers believed that changes would have to be made to avoid a nationwide uprising. In October a relative moderate, Wladyslaw Gomulka, was appointed to the Party's top leadership position. Gomulka insisted that Marshal Rokossovksy be sacked. He also instituted some political reforms. For example, repression of the Catholic Church—historically a very important part of Polish society—was lifted. The activities of Poland's secret police were curtailed. Plans to collectivize Polish farms were abandoned. These developments concerned Soviet leaders, who threatened an invasion. But Gomulka convinced the Kremlin that the reforms didn't signal a rejection of communism or an intention to break with the USSR. They were necessary, he said, for socialism to develop in a manner that would be accepted by the Polish people. The reforms of the "Polish October" proved modest and temporary. But they sowed the seeds for later and more profound change in Poland, as well as other Eastern bloc countries.

The Polish October did have one immediate and dramatic effect: it inspired a popular uprising against Soviet domination in Hungary. The revolution started on October 23, after security forces fired on a crowd of student demonstrators in the capital of Budapest. Soon Hungarian citizens were battling Soviet and Hungarian army forces across the country. For a while, it appeared that the rebels might succeed. Hungary's prime minister and top Communist Party leader fled to the Soviet Union. And on October 31, the Kremlin publicly signaled its willingness to negotiate a withdrawal of Soviet troops from Hungary. That same day, however, Soviet leaders privately decided to crush the uprising with military force. Seventeen Soviet divisions launched a massive attack on November 4. Within a week they had put down the uprising, killing as many as 2,500 Hungarians in the process. Perhaps 200,000 would leave the country as refugees in the aftermath.

Despite the brutal Soviet suppression of the Hungarian Revolution of 1956, a less repressive strain of communism had begun to emerge in Hungary by the mid-1960s. Dubbed "Goulash Communism" after a Hungarian stew, it featured a mix of economic practices. The economy remained predominantly socialistic, with central planning and state control of industry. But some small-scale private businesses were permitted, and limited rights to personal property were recognized. (Yugoslavia tried a similar sort of market socialism.) Though it was by no means an open society, Hungary under Goulash Communism also afforded citizens more personal freedoms

Hungarians cross the border into neighboring Yugoslavia, fall 1956. The brutal Soviet military response to the uprising against Communist rule in Hungary produced nearly 200,000 refugees.

than were allowed in the other Eastern bloc countries. Soviet leaders didn't squelch the Hungarian reforms. Those reforms, in the view of the Kremlin, didn't pose any threat to Soviet control of the Eastern bloc.

The Kremlin reached a different conclusion about reforms introduced in another Eastern bloc country in 1968. During a brief period known as the Prague Spring, Czechoslovakia permitted freedom of speech, freedom of movement, and freedom of the press. The goal of Alexander Dubcek, the leader of Czechoslovakia's Communist Party, was to create a more humane form of communism. The experiment with "socialism with a human face" lasted just six months, however. In August 1968 a half million troops from the USSR and other Warsaw Pact nations invaded Czechoslovakia. Dubcek was arrested, and the reforms were reversed.

In justifying the invasion, Leonid Brezhnev—who had succeeded Khrushchev as the top Soviet leader—offered a rather curious view of the meaning of national sovereignty. "The peoples of the socialist countries and Communist parties certainly do have and should have freedom for determining the ways of advance of their respective countries," Brezhnev said.

> However, none of their decisions should damage either socialism in their country or the fundamental interests of other socialist countries, and the whole working class movement, which is working for socialism.
>
> This means that each Communist Party is responsible not only to its own people, but also to all the socialist countries, to the entire Communist movement.

THE SINO-SOVIET RIFT

If the Soviet Union managed to keep Eastern Europe within its orbit, the same could not be said of China. By the late 1950s, a rift between the world's two largest Communist countries had developed. This split had several causes. One of the most important was Mao Zedong's disapproval of the ideological direction the USSR began to take in the post-Stalin period.

In 1956, three years after Stalin's death, Nikita Khrushchev gave a stunning speech at the 20th Congress of the Communist Party of the Soviet Union. In that speech—which came to be called the Secret Speech, even though it was soon reported publicly—Khrushchev denounced some of Stalin's excesses, especially his purges of Party members and Red Army officers during the 1930s. Khrushchev said that Stalin had created a "cult of personality." He'd portrayed himself as a larger-than-life figure, infallible and almost godlike. Khrushchev condemned this in harsh terms.

Khrushchev began a campaign of "de-Stalinization." Some of this campaign was symbolic. For instance, Stalin's name was removed from buildings, landmarks, and other public places. But there were also substantive policy changes aimed at getting rid of some of the most repressive aspects of Stalin's rule.

Mao Zedong had publicly supported Stalin and was irked by Khrushchev's de-Stalinization campaign. Mao was also outraged by Khrushchev's September 1959 summit with President Eisenhower in Washington, D.C. After their meetings, the two leaders expressed optimism about the chances for better U.S.-USSR relations. Mao interpreted this as evidence the Soviet Union would accept peaceful coexistence with capitalist nations, which he considered an intolerable deviation from Marxist doctrine. In 1961 the Chinese Communist Party branded Khrushchev and the rest of the Soviet leadership as traitors to the cause of communism.

Yet in one significant respect, the CCP—if not Mao Zedong himself—seemed to take to heart what Khrushchev had said in his Secret Speech. In the wake of the disastrous Great Leap Forward, CCP leaders curtailed their own chairman's cult of personality. Mao wasn't criticized directly, as Stalin had been in the USSR. But at the 1962 CCP congress in Beijing, Mao's historical contributions to Chinese communism were downplayed. He was also eased out of his role as China's lead policy maker.

Mao wasn't content to remain on the sidelines. In 1966 he launched a political campaign known as the Great Proletarian Cultural Revolution. Its stated goal was to root out the "bourgeois elements" and "closet capitalists" that, Mao charged, were undermining communism in China. In reality, the Cultural Revolution was mostly a power play: Mao wanted to remove his CCP rivals and regain control. To this end, he encouraged the formation of

Red Guard units, groups of unquestioningly loyal students who denounced authority figures such as Communist Party members, intellectuals, teachers, and parents. Mao also managed to have himself named supreme commander of the Chinese army. His return to power was complete. But the consequences for Chinese society were dire. Industrial production plummeted when factory managers were removed for their supposed bourgeois sympathies. A generation of Chinese youth missed out on an education because schools were closed after their professors were accused of "incorrect" political thinking. Millions of highly trained professionals were forced to do manual labor at "reeducation" camps. Tens of thousands of supposed enemies of communism were killed.

An enormous portrait of Mao Zedong watches over visitors to Beijing's Tiananmen Square. Many Communist leaders, including Mao, have used propaganda to promote themselves as heroic figures who never make mistakes and always act in the best interests of their people. By promoting intense devotion, the leader establishes a "cult of personality" in order to extend his power.

The Cultural Revolution finally ground to an end in 1976, when Mao died. In the years that followed, CCP leaders would chart a more pragmatic and less ideological course directed toward economic development.

CRISES

In late December 1979, Soviet Army units streamed into Afghanistan, a country on the USSR's southwestern border. Communists had seized power there. But they were deeply unpopular among the Afghan people.

Muslim guerrilla fighters had risen up to battle the government, which teetered on the brink of collapse. Kremlin leaders thought the Soviet Army could prop up Afghanistan's Communist regime while restraining its most radical elements.

Soviet forces ran into trouble, however. They were able to control the cities but not Afghanistan's rugged countryside. The rebels staged attacks and then retreated to their mountain hideouts. Soviet forces were unable to dislodge them. The Soviet Army was bogged down. It suffered growing numbers of casualties. Many Soviet citizens grew discontented with the war and with their government.

By the 1980s, the Soviet Union faced other problems besides a drawn-out war. For a long time, the country's economy had been performing badly. Central planning made the economy inefficient. There was little innovation. Workers weren't very productive, and the quality of Soviet-made goods was poor. Eventually, there were chronic shortages of all sorts of goods.

Economic planners directed a large portion of the USSR's resources—perhaps as high as one-quarter—toward the military. This was to keep pace with the United States in the Cold War. But it only worsened the Soviet Union's economic problems.

In the early 1980s, the USSR went through several leadership changes in rapid succession. Leonid Brezhnev died in 1982. Brezhnev's successor, Yuri Andropov, served as general secretary of the Communist Party of the Soviet Union for less than a year and a half before his death. Next came Konstantin Chernenko, who died after just a year in the USSR's top leadership post.

In March 1985 Party leaders elected Mikhail Gorbachev as general secretary. He was considerably younger and less rigid than his predecessors. Gorbachev recognized the need to reform the Soviet system. He tried to ease Cold War tensions with the United States. He introduced measures to restructure the Soviet economy, including loosening state control over some industries. Gorbachev promoted political reforms as well. For the first time, people who weren't Communist Party members were appointed to some government positions. Also, Gorbachev allowed some democratic elections, though not for the top offices. He permitted free speech and a free press, which the Soviet Union had never known.

Gorbachev decided that the Soviet Union would no longer maintain tight control in Eastern Europe. From now on, the Eastern bloc countries would be free to handle their own internal affairs.

Gorbachev didn't undertake all these reforms to get rid of communism. His purpose was to save communism by reforming it. But his plans backfired.

THE COLLAPSE OF COMMUNISM

In Poland, a trade union movement called Solidarity had formed in 1980. The government had outlawed it and arrested its leaders in 1981. But Solidarity's popularity only grew. After nationwide strikes, Poland's Communist government legalized Solidarity in 1989. It also agreed to parliamentary elections. Those elections, held in June, saw Solidarity candidates win decisively. The Communists were swept out of power.

The floodgates of change had opened. In October 1989, Hungary's Communist Party basically voted itself out of existence. It created a multiparty republic.

Soviet leader Mikhail Gorbachev (right) shakes hands with U.S. president Ronald Reagan after signing a nuclear-missile treaty, 1988. During the 1980s Gorbachev attempted to reverse decades of stagnation in the USSR by implementing policies of *glasnost* (openness) and *perestroika* (restructuring). He hoped that the reforms would strengthen the Soviet Union. Instead, the new freedoms undermined the Communist system, and the Soviet republics declared their independence during 1990–91.

In November 1989, East German authorities stopped preventing citizens from going to West Germany. Before the end of the year, the Communist government was gone. Germany was reunified in 1990.

In Czechoslovakia, peaceful demonstrations brought down the Communist government in late November 1989. Democratic elections were held the following year.

In Bulgaria, the Communist government hung on until February 1990. But in the face of massive protests, it too agreed to democratic elections.

In Romania, the revolution was violent, with more than 1,000 people killed. In the end, though, the result was the same. The country's Communist dictator, Nicolae Ceausescu, was toppled, given a hasty trial, and executed.

Even Communist countries not in the Soviet bloc were shaken. Albania, which had left the Warsaw Pact in 1968, saw its Communist regime collapse in 1990. Yugoslavia began breaking apart in civil war the following year.

In the early 1960s, the Communist government of Soviet-controlled East Germany constructed the Berlin Wall. The barrier, designed to prevent East Germans from escaping into U.S.-allied West Germany, became a symbol of the Cold War. In November 1989, as the Communist systems of Soviet bloc were disintegrating, the East German government opened the border with West Germany. Ecstatic crowds celebrated by demolishing the Berlin Wall. Within a year, Germany—divided since the end of World War II—was reunified. Within two years, the Soviet Union had broken into more than a dozen smaller states, none of which retained a Communist system of government.

Inside the Soviet Union, Gorbachev's reforms also had unintended consequences. The newly independent press exposed the government's economic mismanagement. Citizens became more and more resentful of the ruling Communist Party. They weren't satisfied with the freedoms they'd been given. They complained that the pace of reform was too slow. They demanded more.

Free speech also brought into the open some long-simmering ethnic tensions. The Soviet Union was composed of dozens of ethnic groups and nationalities. In previous centuries, most had been brought into the Russian Empire through conquest. And Russians had always dominated the USSR. Members of minority ethnic groups resented this. Now they were able to say so publicly. By 1989–90, ethnic unrest had broken out in a number of regions. In 1990 competitive elections were held to choose parliaments for the soviet socialist republics. In many SSRs, candidates calling for independence from Moscow did well.

Several of the SSR legislatures openly defied Moscow. They declared that their laws took priority over the laws of the Soviet Union.

Gorbachev responded to these developments by drawing up a new treaty of union for the USSR. It would give the SSRs more independence but keep the Soviet Union together.

Hard-line members of the Soviet Communist Party had seen enough. In August 1991, they carried out a coup. They placed Gorbachev under house arrest and issued a statement promising to restore the "honor and dignity" of the Soviet Union.

But people refused to accept the coup. Tens of thousands took to the streets of Moscow. Boris Yeltsin, the newly elected president of the Russian SSR, gave fiery speeches. And in the end, the army refused to move to crush the demonstrators. Within a few days, the coup organizers gave up.

Though Gorbachev was released within several days, he no longer wielded much authority. In late December 1991, the Soviet Union officially dissolved. The former SSRs became independent states. They all quickly abandoned communism.

A FAILED EXPERIMENT?

Today, two decades after the collapse of Soviet communism, only a handful of Communist states remain. The largest—and by far the most important—is the People's Republic of China. China has emerged as an economic powerhouse. But it has done so largely by abandoning Communist economic principles. In the decades after Mao Zedong's death, China embraced free-market reforms. It promoted capitalism. And it experienced rates of sustained economic growth believed to be unequaled in modern history. Millions of Chinese people have been lifted out of poverty and into the middle class.

In spite of this success, many observers doubt that China can continue as a single-party Communist state indefinitely. The Chinese government remains highly repressive. It punishes dissenters harshly. It maintains a vast system for censoring communications, including Internet sites. Still, in recent years the state security apparatus has been unable to prevent the outbreak of violent demonstrations against corrupt CCP officials in various parts of the country. In 2011 even Chinese president Hu Jintao felt compelled to acknowledge the problem of widespread corruption in the Party.

Currently the CCP's main justification for holding a monopoly of power is its management of China's economy. An economic crisis—which is almost inevitable in the long run—will likely trigger social unrest and challenges to the CCP's legitimacy.

Besides China, three other Asian countries remain Communist states. Laos and North Vietnam, like China, have embraced market-based economic reforms. Still, both countries remain poor. North Korea, one of the world's poorest and most isolated nations, has one of the world's most brutal regimes. Supreme leadership in North Korea has been the domain of one family. Kim Il-sung, the country's original Communist dictator, ruled from the end of World War II until his death in 1994. At that point, his son Kim Jong-il took over. Upon his death in 2011, his son Kim Jung-un became North Korea's dictator.

Cuba, the world's only remaining Communist state outside of Asia, has also seen succession based on family ties. In 2008, when an ailing Fidel

Castro stepped aside after nearly 50 years as Cuba's dictator, power passed to his younger brother Raul. The regime's systematic violation of its citizens' basic rights, according to independent human-rights organizations, has continued under the younger Castro.

History has proved Karl Marx's predictions about the inevitable triumph of communism wrong. A class-free society was never created. Under the rule of Communists, no state ever withered away.

In part, the failures of communism have been economic. In complex, industrialized societies, central planning doesn't work well. It makes economies inefficient.

But communism has also fallen short as a basis for governance. Communist states failed to gain the support of their citizens. They survived only through repression. Marx foresaw the "dictatorship of the proletariat." What arose instead was the dictatorship of a ruthless Communist Party.

Traditional symbols of communism—a red banner with a hammer and sickle—adorn this government building in central Pyongyang, the capital of North Korea. In December 2011, Kim Jong-un succeeded his father as ruler of this Communist country.

CHAPTER NOTES

p. 16   "only interpreted the world . . ." Karl Marx, *Theses on Feuerbach*. At Marx/Engels Internet Archive, http://www.marxists.org/archive/marx/works/1845/theses/theses.htm

p. 21:   "The Communists disdain . . ." Karl Marx and Friedrich Engels, *The Communist Manifesto* (New York: Penguin Books, 1981), 120–21.

p. 26:   "The supreme autocratic power . . ." Extracts from the Russian Constitution of April 23, 1906. http://www.shsu.edu/~his_ncp/Const.html

p. 34:   "by all available means . . ." Allan Todd and Sally Waller, *History for the IB Diploma: Authoritarian Single-Party State* (Cambridge, UK: Cambridge University Press, 2011), 117.

p. 36:   "the right of all people . . ." Protocol of Proceedings of Crimea Conference, March 24, 1945. *Modern History Sourcebook: The Yalta Conference, Feb. 1945.* http://www.fordham.edu/halsall/mod/1945YALTA.html

p. 38:   "It must not be imagined . . ." J. V. Stalin, "Questions & Answers to American Trade Unionists: Stalin's Interview with the First American Trade Union Delegation to Soviet Russia." Originally published in *Pravda*, September 15, 1927. Marxists Internet Archives, 2005. http://www.marxists.org/reference/archive/stalin/works/1927/09/15.htm

p. 40:   "[I]t must be the policy . . ." Truman Doctrine—President Harry S. Truman's Address Before a Joint Session of Congress, March 12, 1947. http://avalon.law.yale.edu/20th_century/trudoc.asp

p. 43:   "You have a row of dominoes . . ." David F. Schmitz, *The Tet Offensive: Politics, War, and Public Opinion* (Lanham, MD: Rowman & Littlefield Publishers, 2005), 16.

p. 49:   "The peoples of the socialist . . ." Brezhnev Doctrine: Speech by First Secretary of the Soviet Union Leonid Brezhnev, 13 November 1968. http://www-rohan.sdsu.edu/dept/polsciwb/brianl/docs/1968BrezhnevDoctrine.pdf

CHRONOLOGY

1848: Karl Marx and Friedrich Engels publish *The Communist Manifesto*. The pamphlet urges the world's industrial workers to unite and launch a Communist revolution. Revolutions break out across much of Europe.

1898: The Russian Social Democratic Labor Party (RSDLP) is formed in Minsk.

1903: A dispute at the RSDLP's congress in London causes the party to split into the Menshevik and Bolshevik factions; Lenin leads the Bolsheviks.

1917: Nicholas II, Russia's tsar, is overthrown in March. In November the Bolsheviks seize power and set up the world's first Communist government.

1918–20: The Bolsheviks ("Reds") defeat the "Whites" in a civil war.

1922: On December 30, the Union of Soviet Socialist Republics (USSR) is officially founded. Lenin is its top leader.

1924: Lenin dies in January.

1928: Joseph Stalin is the undisputed leader of the Soviet Union. The First Five-Year Plan for the Soviet economy is adopted.

1932–33: Millions die from starvation as a result of Stalin's rural collectivization campaign. In the Ukraine alone, the death toll reaches an estimated 5 million.

1936–38: Stalin's "Great Purge," a campaign of terror against supposed enemies of the Soviet government, takes place. Up to 1.2 million people are killed, and millions more are imprisoned.

1939: The USSR and Nazi Germany sign a nonaggression pact. World War II begins on September 1.

1941: On June 22, in violation of the nonaggression pact, Germany launches a massive invasion of the Soviet Union.

1945: Germany surrenders in May. Japan's surrender in September brings World War II to an end. Korea is divided along the 38th parallel.

LATE 1940S: Soviet-controlled Communist regimes come to power in Eastern Europe. The Cold War begins.

1949: On October 1, Mao Zedong proclaims the founding of the People's Republic of China.

1950: The Korean War begins in June.

1953: Stalin dies on March 5. The Korean War ends in a stalemate in July.

1956: Nikita Khrushchev begins campaign of de-Stalinization in the USSR. Soviet forces brutally put down the Hungarian Revolution.

1958: China's Great Leap Forward begins.

1959: On January 1, after a three-year guerrilla war, Fidel Castro's revolutionary forces enter Havana and take control of Cuba's government.

1962: After an estimated 30 million Chinese have died from starvation, the Great Leap Forward is abandoned. The Cuban Missile Crisis takes the United States and the USSR to the brink of nuclear war in October.

1968: Soviet forces suppress Czechoslovakia's "Prague Spring" reforms.

1975: Vietnam is unified under Communist Rule. The Khmer Rouge come to power in Cambodia.

1976: Mao Zedong dies.

1979: Soviet forces invade Afghanistan.

1989–90: The Communist governments of Eastern Europe fall.

1991: In December, the USSR officially dissolves.

2010: China becomes the world's second-largest economy.

Bolsheviks demonstrate during a May 1 parade in St. Petersburg's Dvortsovaya Square, 1917. In the late 19th century, members of the working classes in many countries began celebrating May 1 as International Workers' Day. May 1 became an important public holiday in the Soviet Union after the country came under Communist control. The holiday is still observed today in Communist states like China, North Korea, and Cuba.

GLOSSARY

AUTHORITARIAN—favoring blind submission to authority.

CADRES—trained and highly motivated members of a revolutionary party.

CAPITALISM—an economic system that permits the ownership of private property, allows individuals and companies to compete for their own economic gain, and generally lets free market forces determine the price of goods and services.

GENOCIDE—the deliberate and systematic destruction of a racial or cultural group.

IDEOLOGY—a systematic set of principles and goals.

INDOCTRINATION—instruction in the basic principles of a political party or other organization.

NATIONALISM—a sense of national consciousness; promotion of the interests of one's own nation above the interests of other nations.

PRIVATE PROPERTY—in Marxist theory, property capable of producing a profit for its owner.

PROLETARIAT—the class of industrial workers.

SOCIALISM—an economic system that is based on cooperation rather than competition and that utilizes centralized planning and distribution, controlled by the government; in Marxist theory, an intermediate stage between capitalism and communism during which the state—controlled by the proletariat—owns all factories and other places of work, and wages and the distribution of goods are still somewhat unequal.

TOTALITARIAN—relating to a political regime that seeks to exert complete control over citizens' lives.

FURTHER READING

Becker, Jasper. *Hungry Ghosts: Mao's Secret Famine*. New York: Free Press, 1996.

Laqueur, Walter. *The Dream that Failed: Reflections on the Soviet Union*. New York: Oxford University Press USA, 1996.

Pipes, Richard. *Communism: A History*. New York: The Modern Library, 2001.

Szulc, Tad. *Fidel: A Critical Portrait*. New York: Avon, 1986.

INTERNET RESOURCES

http://www.pbs.org/heavenonearth/index.html
The companion website for the PBS documentary Heaven on Earth: The Rise and Fall of Socialism contains short biographies of important figures such as Marx, Lenin, Stalin, and Mao; an illustrated timeline; and more.

http://plato.stanford.edu/entries/marx
The Stanford Encyclopedia of Philosophy entry on Karl Marx.

http://www.coldwar.org
The Cold War Museum offers a multifaceted look at the struggle for global political dominance waged in the latter half of the 20th century by the United States and the Soviet Union.

http://www.chinaview.cn
English web page for Xinhua, China's official wire service.

INDEX

Numbers in bold italics refer to captions.

CONTRIBUTORS

Senior Consulting Editor **TIMOTHY J. COLTON** is Morris and Anna Feldberg Professor of Government and Russian Studies and is the chair of the Department of Government at Harvard University. His books include *The Dilemma of Reform in the Soviet Union* (1986); *Moscow: Governing the Socialist Metropolis* (1995), which was named best scholarly book in government and political science by the Association of American Publishers; *Transitional Citizens: Voters and What Influences Them in the New Russia* (2000); and *Popular Choice and Managed Democracy: The Russian Elections of 1999 and 2000* (with Michael McFaul, 2003). Dr. Colton is a member of the editorial board of World Politics and Post-Soviet Affairs.

RUDOLPH T. HEITS, a freelance writer originally from Texas, is the author of several books for young adults.

PICTURE CREDITS: IMS Communications, Ltd.: 51; Library of Congress: 6, 9, 10, 30, 33, 60; National Archives: 35; © 2012 Photos.com, a division of Getty Images: 18, 20, 23, 28; courtesy Ronald Reagan Library: 53; used under license from Shutterstock, Inc.: 1, 57; jorisvo / Shutterstock.com: 43; U.N. Photo: 41, 48; U.S. Department of Defense: 54.